COMPU

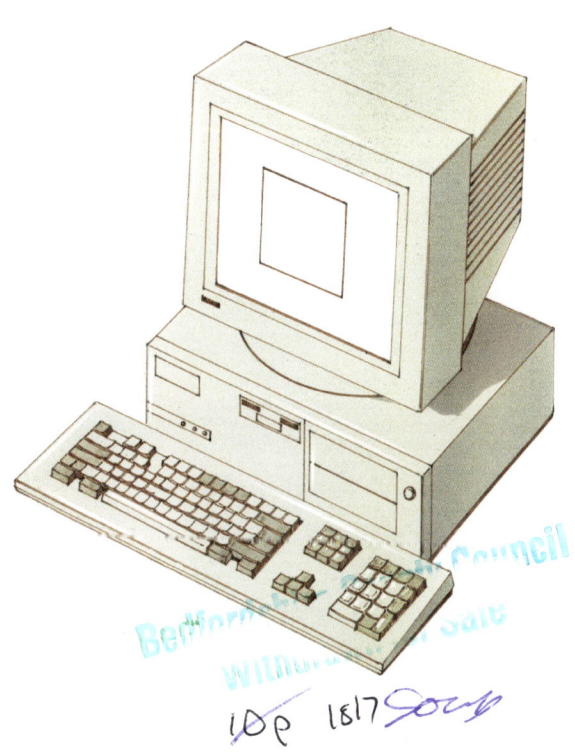

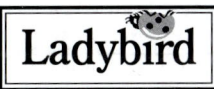

written by Carole Hay
illustrated by Studio Boni/Galante
and Lorenzo Cecchi

Ladybird

CONTENTS

J oou HAY

WHAT IS A COMPUTER?

A computer is a machine that stores and **processes** information. Just as a mincer processes food, a computer processes 'raw' words, or pictures, into other things, for example, a storybook.

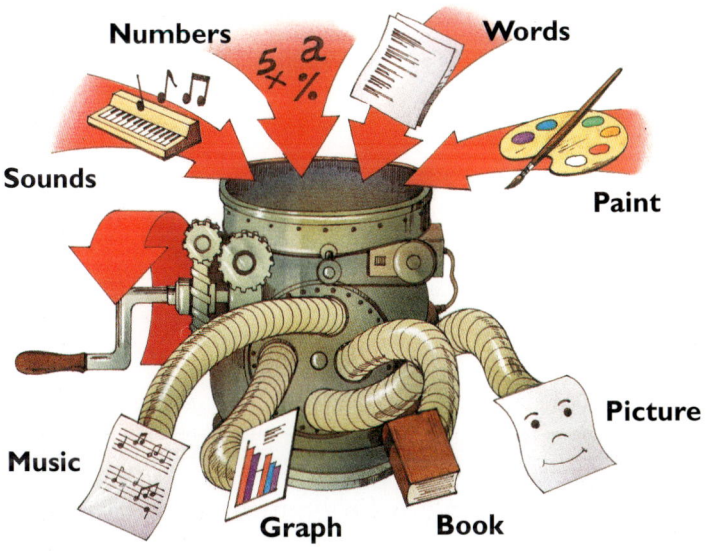

Functions of a computer

People **input** information into the computer. This **data** can be words, numbers or drawings, for example. The computer processes the data using instructions that people have input into its **memory**.

The result is **output** to the computer screen which can be printed. A computer's memory is important because it allows the computer to store different sets of instructions and data for the different jobs that it does.

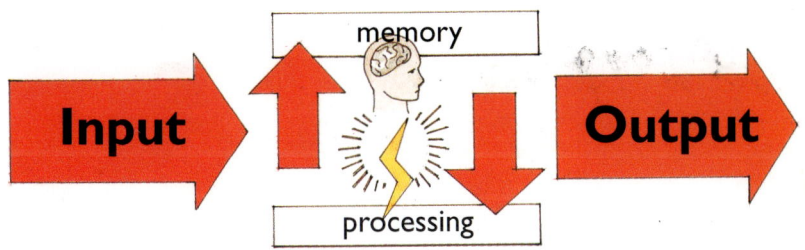

HOW IT ALL BEGAN

As long as people have needed to count and calculate sums, they have been inventing tools to help make these things easier and faster. Today's powerful computers can do 'number crunching' at lightning speed. What were some of their ancestors?

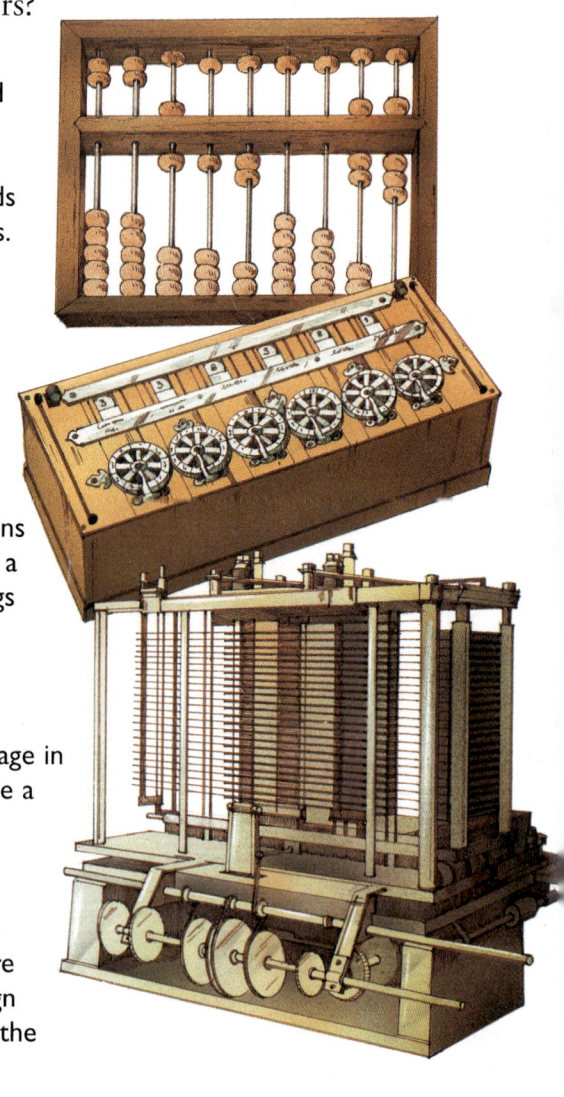

Abacus
The abacus has been used for thousands of years to speed up calculations. To help with arithmetic, beads are slid along parallel rods. It is still used today in some places.

Early calculators
The world's first calculating machine was invented in 1642 by a Frenchman named Pascal. Like the abacus, calculations were done by hand, using a system of interlocking cogs and pulleys.

Analytic engine
The analytic engine was designed by Charles Babbage in 1833. He wanted to create a machine to do jobs that were boring for people. The machine was never built in Babbage's lifetime, but modern computers are based on his original design and he is remembered as the 'father of the computer'.

First electronic computer

The Electronic Numerical Integrator and Calculator (ENIAC) was developed in 1946 to calculate artillery firing tables for the American army. As it turned out, the machine was capable of being programmed with different sets of instructions to do many other tasks as well. ENIAC was the first totally electronic computer, using over 18,000 valves to send electrical signals. The machine was very large and filled an entire room, but it could do an impressive 5,000 calculations per second.

THE SHRINKING COMPUTER

The valves used in the first electronic computers were thousands of times faster than the mechanical switches used previously. But valves were very expensive, fragile and could easily become overheated. The invention of the transistor revolutionised the making of computers. The transistor was a kind of switch that did the same job as a valve, but was smaller, faster and cheaper. As new materials were used to make transistors, they could be made even smaller and eventually packaged together on **microchips**.

7 cm

Valve   **Transistor**   **Microchip**

Relative sizes
A valve, transistor and microchip are shown in their real size, relative to each other. Transistors are about half the size of old-fashioned valves, and microchips are far smaller than transistors.

THE PLASTIC CASE
A microchip is kept in a plastic case with a cover to protect it. It is connected to the rest of the computer by many metal pins that look like a spider's legs.

Metal pin

Microchip

Plastic case

MICROCHIPS

Microchips are about the size of a child's fingernail. They are made from very thin slices, or 'chips', of a mineral called silicon. Each chip is only 0.1 of a millimetre thick. A many-layered pattern of electrical pathways or circuits, too small to be seen by the naked eye, is etched on the surface of each individual microchip.

An enlarged microchip

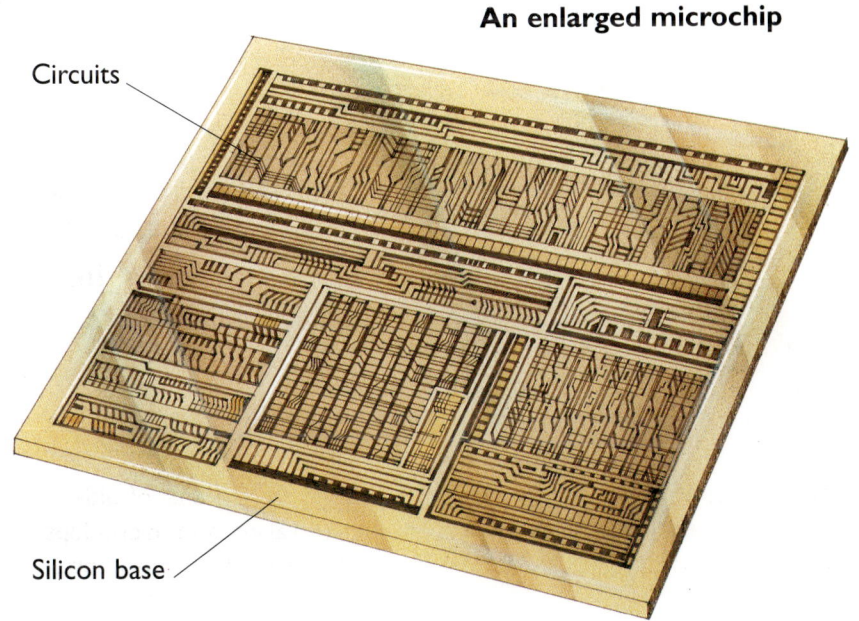

Circuits

Silicon base

The one-chip computer

There are different types of chip to perform different jobs within a computer. However, it is also possible to combine these functions on one chip. This type of chip is specialised to do a particular job. It can be built into all kinds of machines to control them and provide added information. Modern televisions, videos, calculators and cars have all become faster and more efficient machines with the addition of microchips.

ALL DIFFERENT SIZES

The first computers were expensive and needed a lot of space. They were only used by governments and large businesses. Nowadays, computers come in all shapes and sizes – from enormous **mainframe**s that have to be kept in special temperature controlled rooms, to portable computers that fit in the palm of your hand.

Mainframes

Mainframe computers are the largest and most powerful computers available. They can serve hundreds of people and do many jobs at the same time.

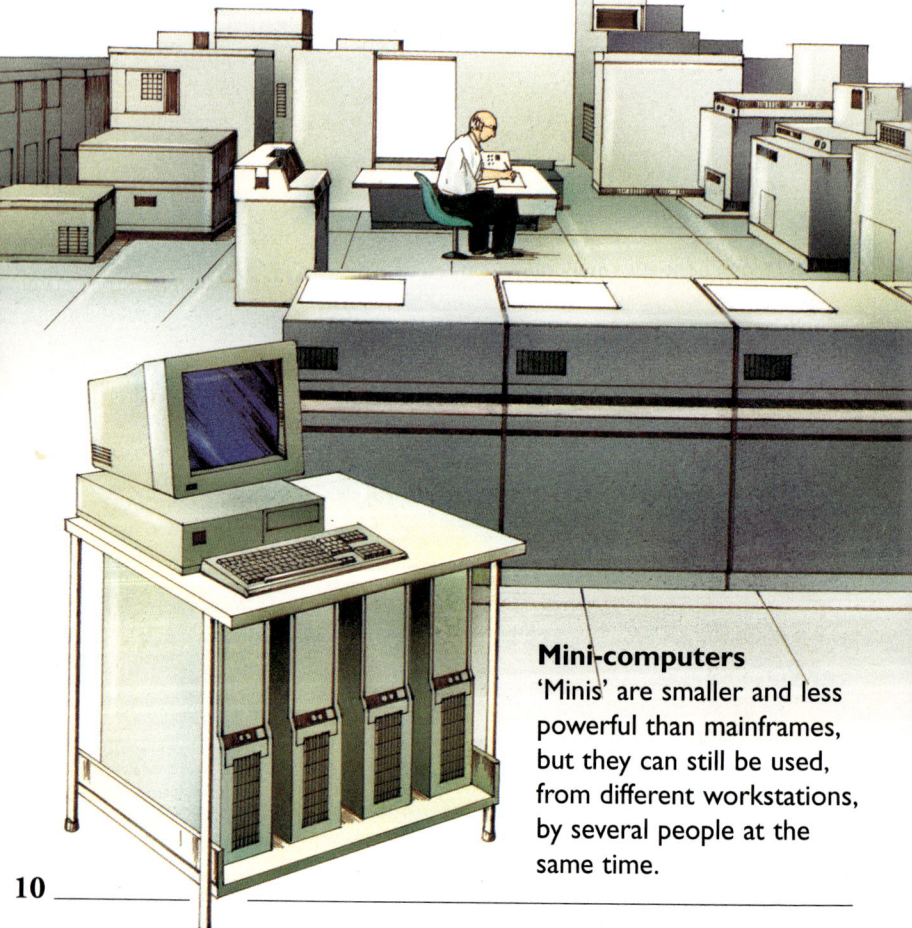

Mini-computers

'Minis' are smaller and less powerful than mainframes, but they can still be used, from different workstations, by several people at the same time.

Networks

Local Area **Networks** (LANs) are small groups of computers linked together by wires or cables in a single office, building, or closely grouped buildings.

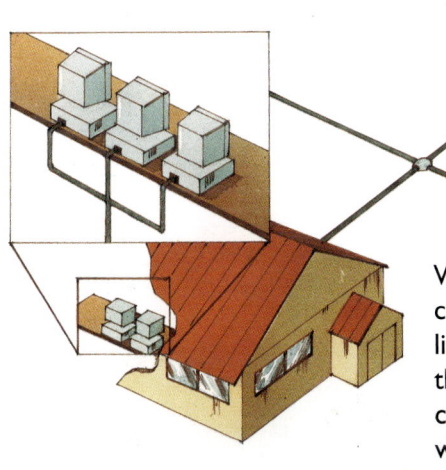

Wide Area Networks (WANs) connect all types of computers, linking towns and cities across the world. WANs enable computers to communicate with each other over long distances, using telephone lines, radio waves, microwaves and satellites.

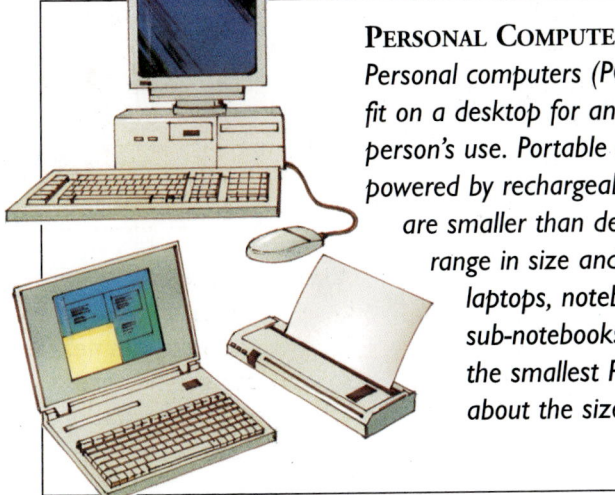

PERSONAL COMPUTERS

Personal computers (PCs) are made to fit on a desktop for an individual person's use. Portable computers are powered by rechargeable batteries and are smaller than desktop PCs. They range in size and can be called laptops, notebooks and sub-notebooks. Palmtops are the smallest PCs and are only about the size of a calculator.

COMPUTER HARDWARE

Input devices are used to input information into the computer. Results of computer processing are output through output devices. The keyboard is the most common input device, and the screen, or monitor, the most common output device. All these devices are called computer **hardware**. Hardware is the 'hard' computer equipment you can see and touch.

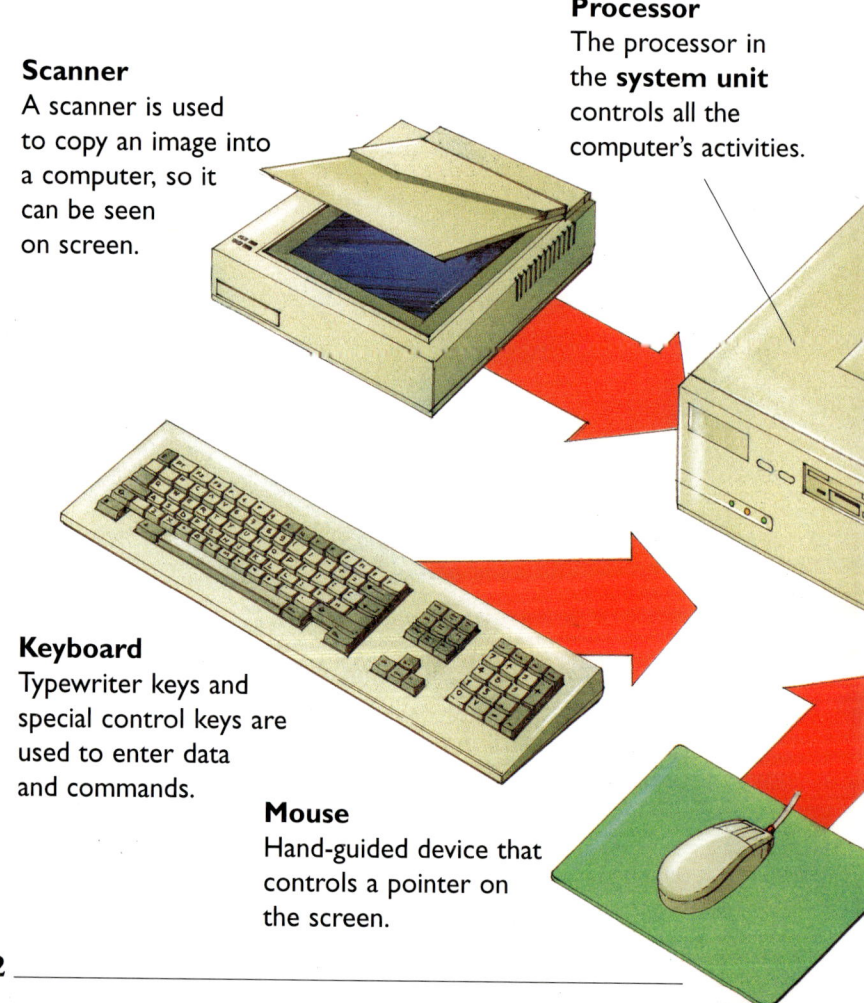

Scanner
A scanner is used to copy an image into a computer, so it can be seen on screen.

Processor
The processor in the **system unit** controls all the computer's activities.

Keyboard
Typewriter keys and special control keys are used to enter data and commands.

Mouse
Hand-guided device that controls a pointer on the screen.

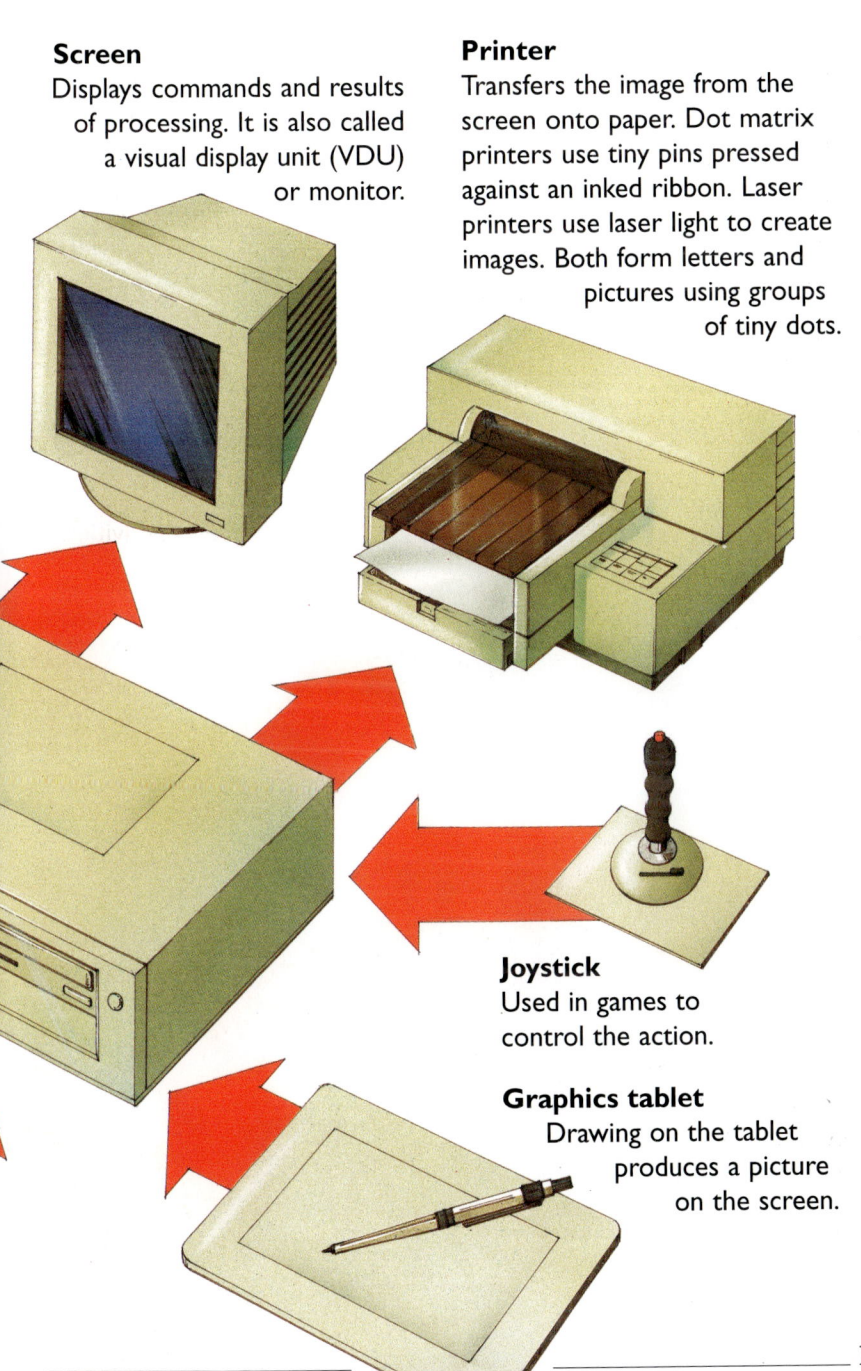

Screen

Displays commands and results of processing. It is also called a visual display unit (VDU) or monitor.

Printer

Transfers the image from the screen onto paper. Dot matrix printers use tiny pins pressed against an inked ribbon. Laser printers use laser light to create images. Both form letters and pictures using groups of tiny dots.

Joystick

Used in games to control the action.

Graphics tablet

Drawing on the tablet produces a picture on the screen.

HOW IT WORKS

Because a computer uses electricity to work, everything it processes must be translated into electrical signals. The **binary** system of numbers uses only 0s and 1s so is an ideal system for this job. With these two digits, program instructions, letters, numbers, symbols, pictures and colours can all be coded into electricity.

Binary code
The **ASCII** (pronounced ask-kee) standard is a special code used by computers to designate eight binary digits (one **byte**) to each keyboard character. When a key is pressed, it is translated inside the computer into its ASCII code. Below are the ASCII codes for 'A' and '5'

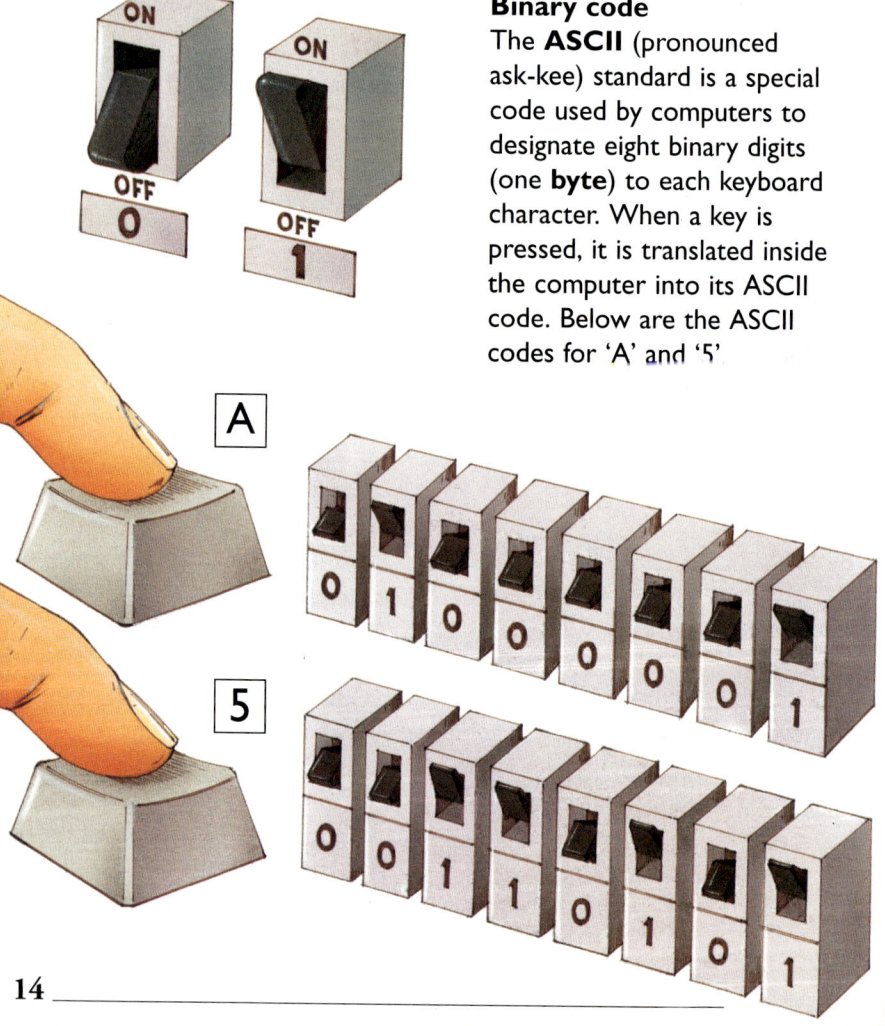

1. Input human language into the computer.

2. Translated inside the computer into binary code.

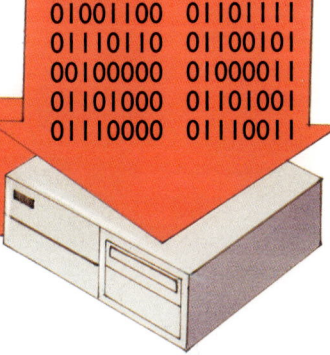

3. Output to the screen translated back to human language.

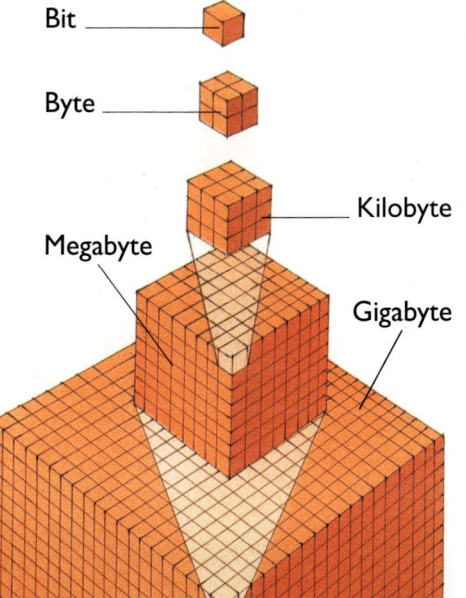

Bit

Byte

Kilobyte

Megabyte

Gigabyte

Bits and bytes
A bit is one binary digit, either 0 or 1. A byte is 8 bits.

A kilobyte is roughly one thousand bytes (1,024). A megabyte is roughly one million bytes (1,048,576). This is about 500 pages of text.

A gigabyte is roughly one billion bytes (1,073,741,824). This is about half a million pages of text.

PROGRAMS

Computer hardware is useless without programs or **software**. These are the step-by-step instructions a computer must be given for doing a particular job. Complicated tasks are broken down into hundreds and thousands of simple steps. Only one small step is done at a time, but the computer works so fast that millions of steps add up to useful work in a matter of seconds.

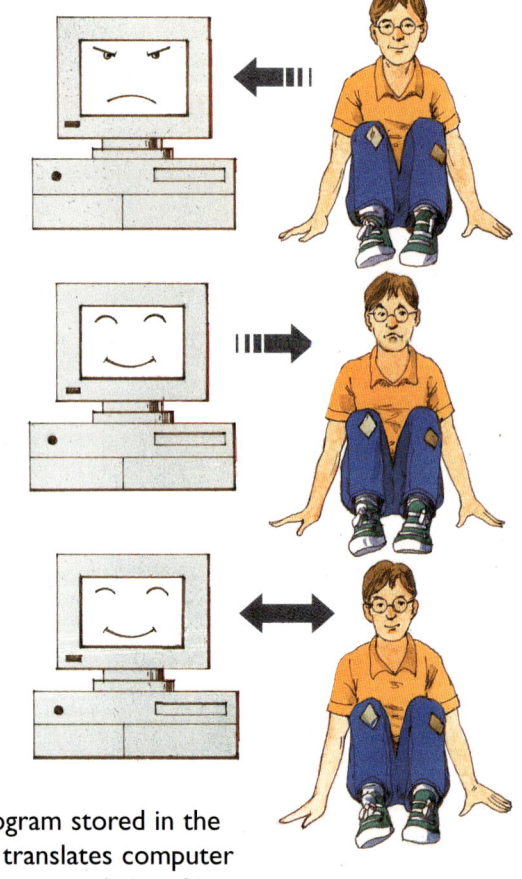

'Smile'
Words are easy for us to understand, but not for a computer.

'00110010'
Binary code is easy for the computer to understand, but not for us.

01 PRINT "SMILE"
Commands written in a programming language, for example, BASIC, are easier than binary for us to understand.

Interpreter
The interpreter is a program stored in the computer's memory. It translates computer programming language commands into binary code that the computer can understand.

THE OPERATING SYSTEM

The operating system is a special program needed by all computers. It contains instructions needed to start the computer and manage tasks for programs. Part of the operating system remains in the memory all the time the computer is running. Different machines have different operating systems, but manufacturers are developing new systems that can be used by all computers.

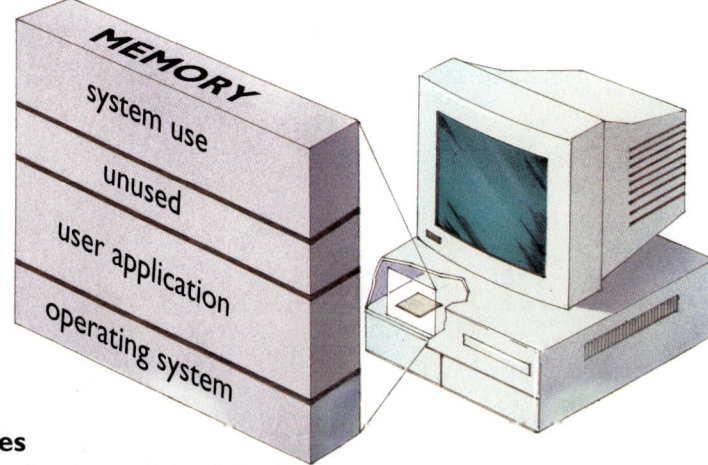

Files
One important job of the operating system is to manage information. This information is kept in files. Programs and data are kept in separate files and given a name. Files are usually stored on a disk and are read into memory when needed.

Finding a file
Finding a file from a computer screen is like opening a filing cabinet, and selecting which one you want.

THE SYSTEM UNIT

The system unit contains all parts of a computer needed to store and process data. Buttons, switches, sockets and disk drives connect the inner processing power to other hardware, like a mouse and screen.

Disk drives
Programs and data are stored on disks which must be inserted into the disk drive so that their information can be used by the computer.

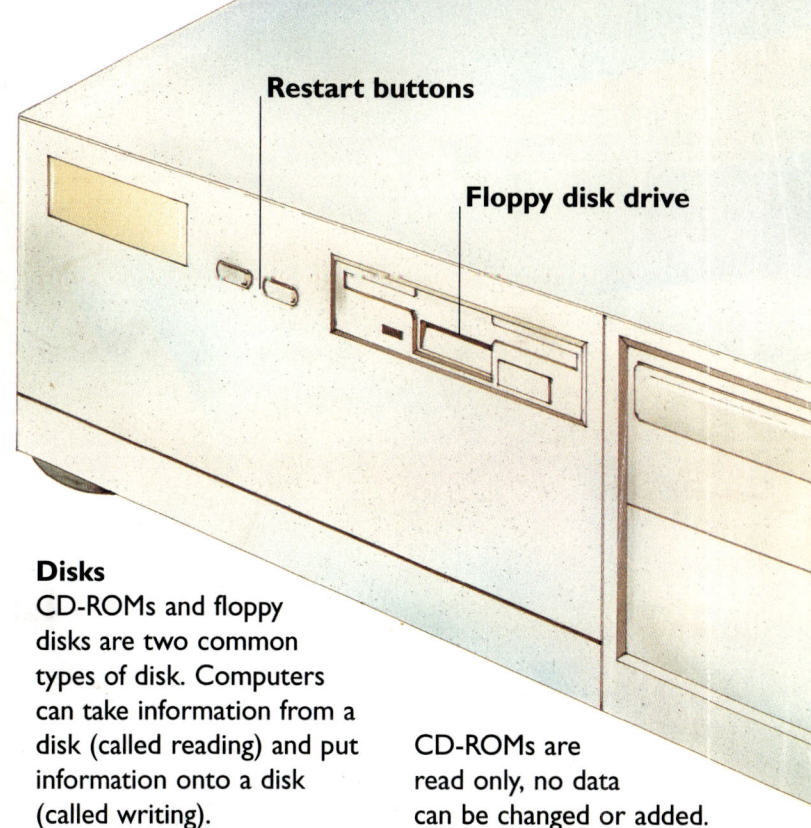

Disks
CD-ROMs and floppy disks are two common types of disk. Computers can take information from a disk (called reading) and put information onto a disk (called writing).

CD-ROMs are read only, no data can be changed or added.

17   18

INSIDE THE COMPUTER

The Central Processing Unit (CPU) of a personal computer has more processing power than one of the early, room-sized computers. The system unit has several components – the processor chip, clock, memory chips, input/output circuits and storage devices which are connected together to achieve the many tasks the computer does.

Floppy disk

Capacity
The full capacity of a floppy disk is 1.4 megabytes (about 700 pages of text). CD-ROM disks can hold over 400 times this amount.

CD-ROM disk

Storage
Storage is necessary to keep data and programs over long periods, when the machine is turned off. Hard disks, floppy disks and CD-ROMs are the main type of storage devices commonly used today.

Memory
Memory in the computer is needed to store the machine's basic instructions and to keep programs and data available for use by the CPU.

Read Only Memory (ROM)
Microchips contain instructions which include most of the system's basic input/output system, instructions for starting the computer and managing the flow of information between various parts of the computer. So when the computer is switched off, the ROM is not erased.

Random Access Memory (RAM)
Chips with RAM temporarily store data and program instructions while the CPU needs them. RAM is erased when the computer is switched off, so any work that will be needed again must be saved onto a disk.

BACK VIEW

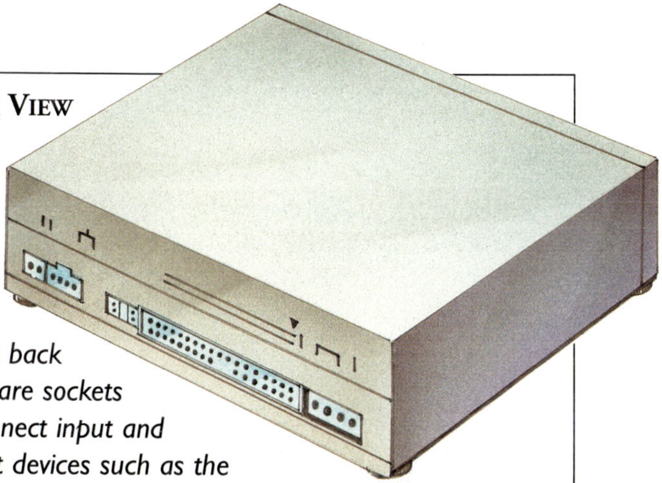

At the back there are sockets to connect input and output devices such as the keyboard and printer. The fan vent lets air ventilate the inside of the system unit.

CD-ROM drive

Power button

Drive motor
Each disk drive has a small electric motor which spins the disk, making all of its sections available to the computer.

23

COMPUTERS ALL AROUND US

Computers began as super 'number-crunchers', able to calculate complicated maths at high speed. They were mainly used by the military, in space flight and in finance. Now, computers are found almost everywhere, for example, in an automatic camera.

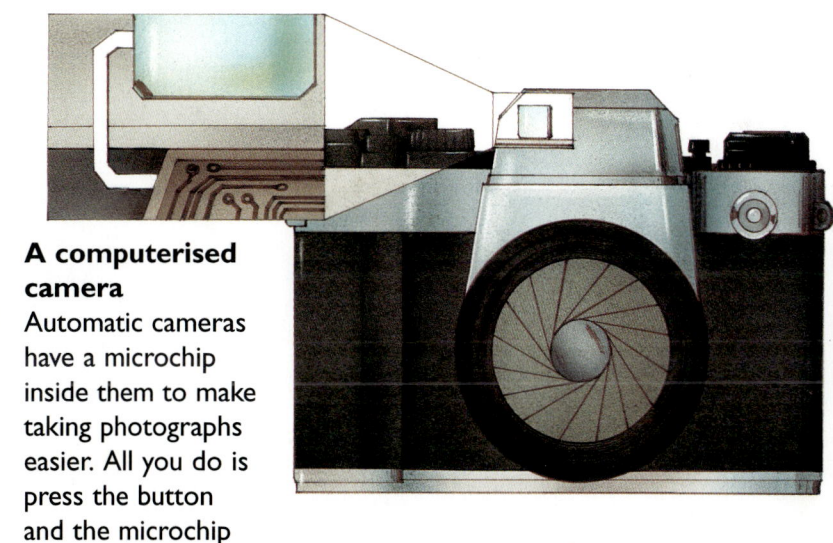

A computerised camera
Automatic cameras have a microchip inside them to make taking photographs easier. All you do is press the button and the microchip does the rest.

A light sensor in the camera sends light readings to the camera's microchip. Using these readings, the chip outputs signals to control the amount of light the camera lets in, in order to expose the film correctly.

24

Hard disk
A non-removable stack of disks in an airtight case. Like a floppy, the hard disk can be read and written to, but it is faster and has a much larger storage capacity (from 20 megabytes to 9 gigabytes).

Expansion slots
These are available to expand the power of the computer and increase its capacity to do things. Expansion cards can be put in the slots for additional sound and picture output.

MORE AND MORE MEMORY

Advances in technology mean that computer memory chips are more powerful and cheaper to produce than ever before. Also, disks are being made that can hold more information. This means that personal computers often include a CD-ROM drive for playing CD-ROMs and speakers that produce realistic sound effects.

Sound
Computers are often fitted with a special converter to output sound. Sound is input through a microphone. The converter changes sound waves, that our ears respond to, into digital sound – a signal made up of bits (0s and 1s) instead of waves. This is a very useful feature. Most modern music uses computers to enhance and modify the original sound input.

Pictures
Computers cannot draw or create pictures in the same way as we can. Computers with powerful memories can be programmed to display pictures – imaginary ones that a programmer visualises. This is done by giving instructions to each **pixel** – one of the tiny dots that make up a screen.

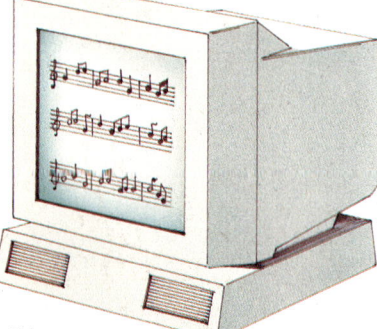

22

Computers everyday

Computers are a vital part of everyday life. They are used in: 1. Sea navigation, 2. Space flight, 3. Cash dispensers, 4. Traffic lights, 5. Medicine, 6. Weather stations, 7. Air traffic control, 8. **Simulation**, 9. Police forces, 10. Communication, 11. Robotics.

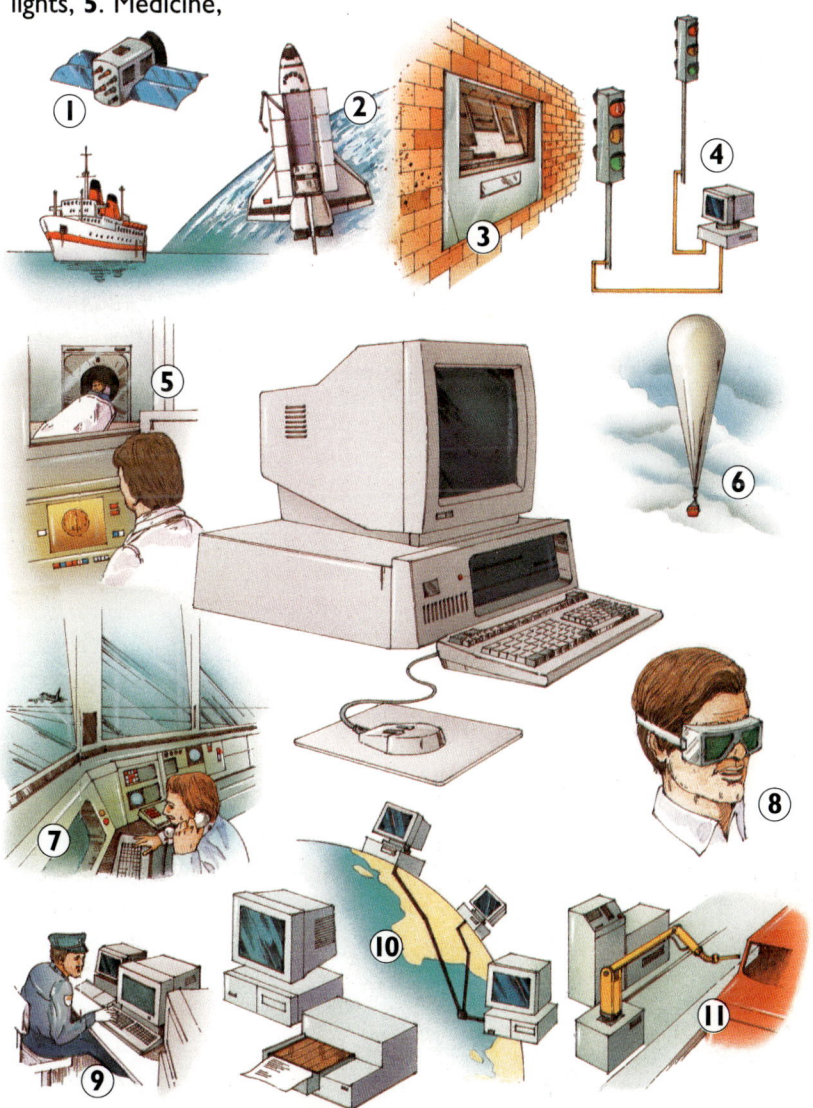

ANOTHER LOOK AT PROGRAMMING

People have the ability to do, or think of, lots of things at the same time. Computers, however, can only do one task at a time. Therefore, to communicate with a computer, people need to break their instructions down into small, logical pieces that tell the machine exactly what to do in a step-by-step way.

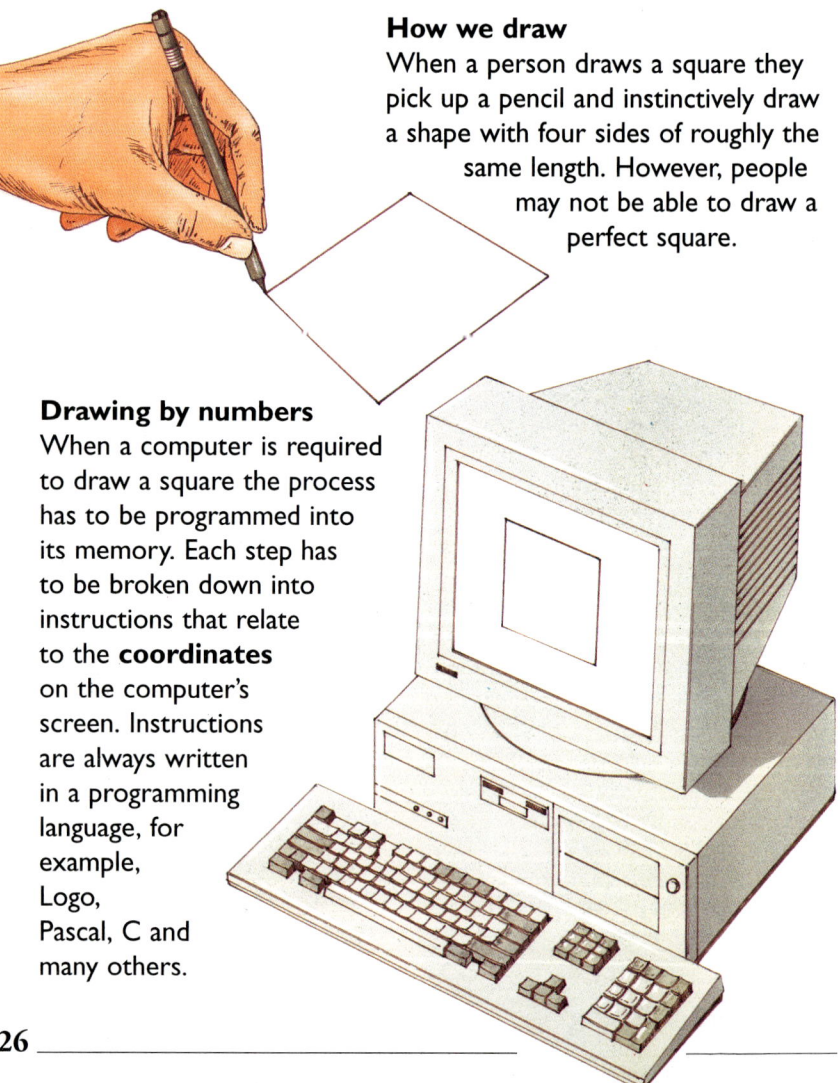

How we draw
When a person draws a square they pick up a pencil and instinctively draw a shape with four sides of roughly the same length. However, people may not be able to draw a perfect square.

Drawing by numbers
When a computer is required to draw a square the process has to be programmed into its memory. Each step has to be broken down into instructions that relate to the **coordinates** on the computer's screen. Instructions are always written in a programming language, for example, Logo, Pascal, C and many others.

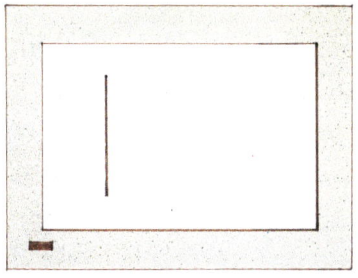

Forward 100mm

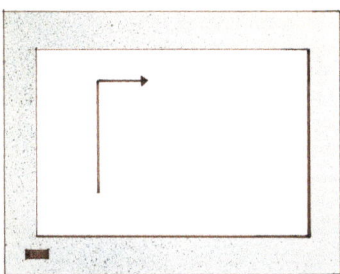

Right 90°

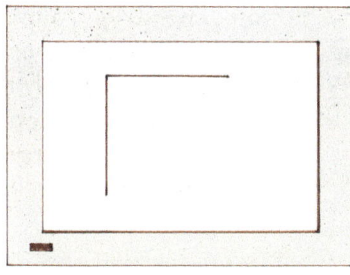

Forward 100mm

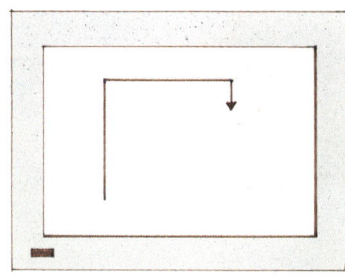

Right 90°

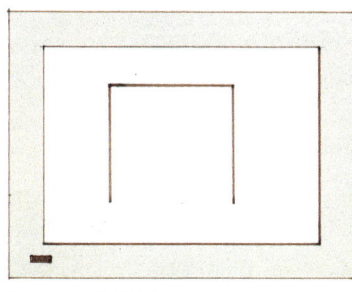

Forward 100mm

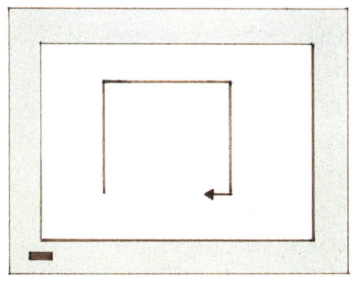

Right 90°

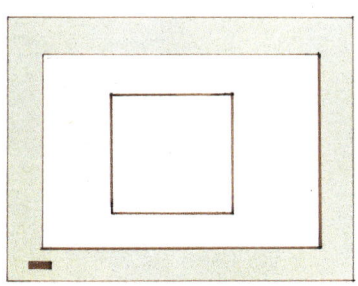

Forward 100mm

Once the program has been placed into the computer's memory, it can be used over and over again to reproduce any number of identical squares. The original square can also be changed countless times. For example, you may want to rotate it, to form a diamond.

LEARNING AND PLAYING

Computers are being used more and more in schools and at home as learning tools. They help people to learn at their own speed and ability. There are many kinds of software available for teaching anything from maths and biology to learning to read. Even very young children can quickly learn how to use a computer.

LEARNING IS FUN
*The computer provides a friendly, **interactive** way of learning. Some software uses popular cartoon characters, games and puzzles to enable children to learn the alphabet or do simple sums. The computer corrects mistakes and rewards you when you get things right.*

Computer games

Computer games often use the latest developments in graphics and animation. Simulation games transport the player into scenes that mimic the real world. For example, being a pilot or the mayor of a city. In adventure games you help the hero discover tools and solve problems. Sports, racing cars and arcade action games are also popular.

Multimedia

Multimedia software contains words, pictures, sounds and films. This software usually comes on a CD-ROM. Many CD-ROMs are interactive – you take part in what happens on the screen and choose what you want to see. A multimedia book can be stored on a CD-ROM. The advantage of this is that you can look things up easily and print out what you want.

SAFETY AND SECURITY

As more and more people need to use computers regularly, health problems related to poor working conditions have appeared. People who work for long periods at a computer need adjustable equipment to help maintain good posture. They need to take frequent breaks to prevent strains to the eyes, neck, back and wrists.

User-friendly

An adjustable keyboard with wrist rests helps make the typist comfortable.

Protecting data

The write-protect tab of a floppy disk can be pushed up to make the disk 'read only'. This prevents important data from being accidentally erased.

Write-protect tab

Care of disks

All floppy disks and CD-ROMs should be kept in enclosed containers to prevent damage by dust or spills. They should be kept at room temperature, away from direct sunlight and magnets.

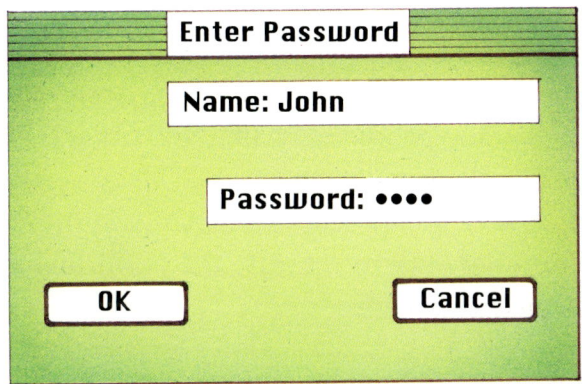

Passwords

Passwords are used to protect programs and data. When the program starts, the password screen is the first screen displayed. The user types in his or her own private password. It is not displayed on screen. This prevents other people from seeing it. If the password entered is correct, the program starts. If not, the program cannot be used.

Viruses

Viruses are programs hidden in other programs that alter files without the user's knowledge. They are passed from one computer to another by 'infected' floppy disks. A virus may just display a silly message but, more seriously, it sometimes interferes with the computer's ability to work. When you insert a new disk, its files should be checked by anti-virus software before loading them onto your computer.

ONLINE

The computer network revolution began in the 1980s and is still going on. Local area networks are a convenient way for people to share data, programs and expensive equipment such as printers. There is now a wide range of accessories that can be added on to a computer or a network to increase the performance and range of a computer's uses.

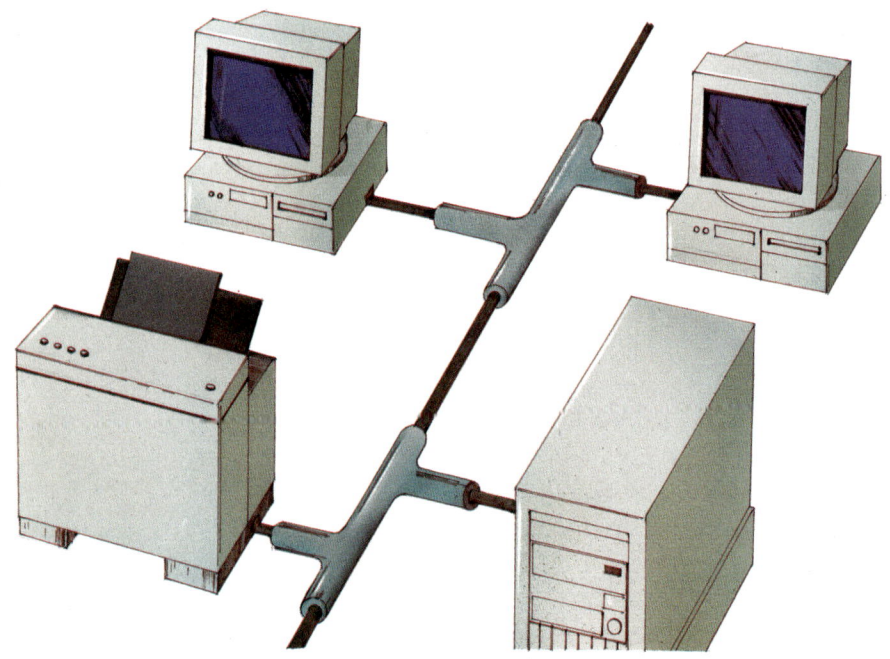

Electronic mail
Electronic mail (E-mail) is a fast and easy way to send and receive messages and information to other people without leaving your desk.

Modems
A modem is a device that can be attached to your computer to allow you to communicate with other computers, either locally, or over long distances using telephone lines.

Internet

Sometimes known as the information super-highway or cyberspace, the Internet is a worldwide network, connecting millions of computer users. Anyone with a home computer and a modem can connect to the Internet by opening an account with a service provider. This could be a commercial company or a university, for example. The Internet has an enormous range of information areas, called sites.

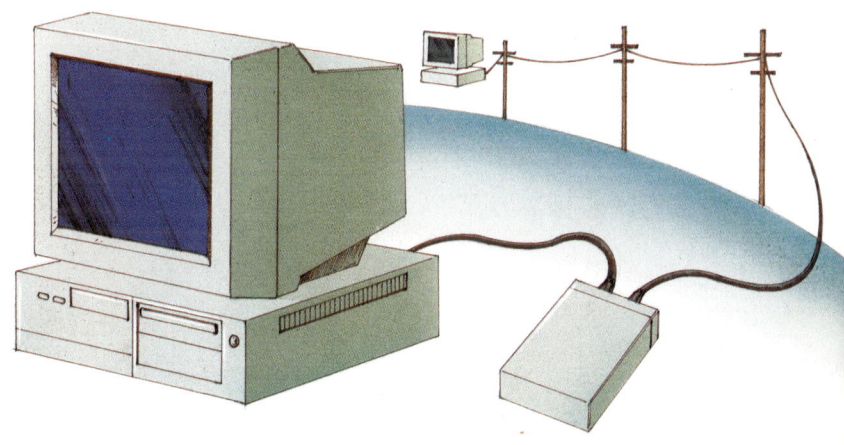

ONLINE SERVICES

Once you're connected to the Internet, there are limitless possibilities: you could join a chat-group, send messages to users in other countries, or try out new games and puzzles. Services for children include stories, jokes and ideas from other children all over the world.

COMPUTERS AND THE FUTURE

Computers you talk to, computer screens worn on contact lenses, interactive TV, videophones, wireless networks... may sound like science fiction but will be here in the near future.

Teleworking
More people will be able to work from home or remote offices using networks to connect them with a central office base.

Teleshopping
Businesses on the network and interactive TV will demonstrate products and allow you to buy at the press of a button.

VIDEO-CONFERENCING
High quality 'video-conferencing' is becoming available on PC-networked systems.
You can see the person you are talking to on a screen at the same time as working on a shared document.

Virtual reality

Computers can now be programmed to create realistic three dimensional worlds. This is called virtual reality (VR). Using headsets, experts such as pilots and surgeons use VR to practise complex jobs. Many other jobs we need to learn will be able to take advantage of this technology in the future.

The office you wear

Imagine: a powerful computer strapped to your wrist; no keyboard, you talk to your computer and it talks back; a screen clips to your head or your glasses; all connected to a worldwide network via a mobile phone, giving you access to limitless information. Computer scientists promise these things are on the way.

RICH AND POOR

Computer technology brings knowledge and opportunities at a staggering rate. Poorer, developing countries lag far behind in access to this technology. Can this gap be bridged so that computer technology is spread more evenly?

AMAZING COMPUTER FACTS

- **Home entertainment**
One CD-ROM disk can hold
70 minutes of full-screen,
full-motion video with
CD-quality sound.

- **More chips please**
In 1971, the microprocessor
chip used in the first
successful PC had 6,000
transistors. The pentium chip
introduced in 1993 uses 3,100,000 transistors.

- **Colour magic** Colour printers use a mixture of only four
different colours (cyan, magenta, yellow and black) to create
the thousands of colours printed onto the page.

- **Football crazy** Robo-kicker is a robot that kicks a football
like a professional player. It can take a penalty kick every
15 seconds and is used to test football boots and balls.

- **Photo opportunity** Photographs can be scanned and
saved onto a photo-CD or a floppy disk by photo developers.
You can then insert your own photographs into computer
documents.

- **Virtually amazing** In a film released in 1996, the star
has a 3-D computer-generated double that can be manipulated
by a PC to perform stunts and do
battles in virtual reality inside
the computer.

- **Doctor robot** Robots
can be programmed to
perform some surgical
operations. The doctor
inputs the data it needs
to start and then monitors
the robot's progress
on a screen.

GLOSSARY

ASCII A computer code that uses binary numbers to represent letters and numbers.

Binary The number system used by computers. It has only two digits, 0 and 1.

Byte A unit of measurement used to indicate the storage power of a computer – usually referred to in kilobytes, megabytes and gigabytes.

Coordinates A set of numbers used to specify the location of a point on screen.

Data Information used by a computer.

Hardware Hard computer equipment that you can touch.

Input Data entered into the computer by the user.

Interactive A method of learning or playing games that allows for the exchange of information between a computer and a user.

Mainframe A massive computer used for processing very large amounts of data. Hundreds of PCs can be linked to a mainframe so that many people can use its power at one time.

Memory The part of a computer that stores the instructions and data it needs to do its job.

Microchip A complete circuit containing microscopic transistors and other electronic parts on a single silicon chip.

Multimedia A combination of text, pictures, sound, and video in one piece of software.

Network A group of computers connected together to send, receive and share information with one another.

Output Results of computer processing sent back to a user.

Pixel One of the thousands of dots that make up a screen. The more pixels there are, the better the picture quality.

Processing Work done by a computer to complete a task.

Simulation A working model of a real thing.

Software The instructions a computer must be given to enable it to do a particular task.

System unit The main part of a computer where data is stored and processed.

INDEX *(Entries in **bold** refer to an illustration)*